Published by Creative Education
123 South Broad Street, Mankato, Minnesota 56001
Creative Education is an imprint of The Creative Company

Designed by Stephanie Blumenthal
Production Design by Tamarin Graphics

Photographs by Michele Burgess, Anthony R. Dalton, John Elk III,
Galyn C. Hammond, Scott Heinrichs, Craig Lovell, Ardella Reed, Root Resources,
Leonard L. Rue III, Eugene Schulz, Carol Simowitz, Ingrid Mårn Wood

Library of Congress Cataloging-in-Publication Data

Richardson, Adele, 1966–
India / by Adele Richardson
p. cm. — (Let's Investigate)
Includes glossary and index
Summary: Examines the history, landscape, wildlife, people, and
weather of the nation of India.
ISBN 1-58341-031-7
1. India—Juvenile literature. [1. India.] I. Title. II. Series.
III. Series: Let's Investigate (Mankato, Minn.)
DS407.R54   1999
954—dc21   99-10886

First edition

2 4 6 8 9 7 5 3 1

INDIA

ADELE RICHARDSON

Creative Education

INDIA

MONEY

India's unit of money, called the rupee, *is similar to the dollar in that it is divided into 100* paise *(like pennies). About 30 rupees is equal to one U.S. dollar.*

Above, traditional Indian paper-mâché puppets Right, Tomb of Humayun, built from 1557 to 1565

India is a large, beautiful country located on the southern part of the Asian continent. It is one-third the size of the United States, yet is the second-most populated place on Earth. Only China has more people. This land of scorching deserts, high mountains, and rolling **plains** is filled with a variety of plants and animals, some very rare. India's people must work hard to survive, and many live in poverty. Despite this, India has made much progress in the last 50 years toward improving life for its people.

INDIA

TURTLE

Once a year in Gahirmatha state, millions of baby sea turtles hatch from eggs and leave their nests at the same time, then head into the Bay of Bengal.

Above, a temple painting Right, the Shore Temple at Mahabalipuram near Madras, India

LAND AND CLIMATE

Along the northern part of the country are the Himalayas, the world's highest mountains. Other mountain ranges wind down both sides of the country, called the Western and Eastern Ghats. The word *Ghat* means "step." The Vindya Mountains run east from the Arabian Sea and separate the northern part of the country from the **peninsula**. India's highest mountain, Kanchenjunga, rises 28,809 feet (8,781 m) high and is part of the Himalayan range.

India shares its northern borders with seven other countries: Bangladesh, Burma, Bhutan, Nepal, China, Afghanistan, and Pakistan. The southern part of the country is a large, triangle-shaped peninsula; the very tip juts into the Indian Ocean. On the west coast is the Arabian Sea; the Bay of Bengal laps on the east. Up and down both coastlines are thick jungles and **rain forests** where many animals live.

7

In India, elephants are often used for work; they are trained by men called mahouts

INDIA
SHRINE

Stupas are memorial structures built by people of the Buddhist religion. Within each shrine there may be a small statue of the person for whom the stupa was built.

8

Above, Buddhist stupas Right, rice is a major crop in the Himachal Pradesh Kais village in the Kulu Valley

outh of the towering Himalayas is the largest plain in the world, called the Gangetic Plain. As snow melts on the mountains, water flows down to the plains, carrying with it rich minerals to fertilize the soil. A lot of farming is done on these plains because the ground is **fertile** and can grow many plants.

Two of India's longest rivers flow through the northern plains. The Brahmaputra River is more than 1,800 miles (2,898 km) long, and the Ganges stretches for nearly 1,560 miles (2,511 km). These rivers, like the melting snow, bring many nutrients to the farmlands.

The Deccan **Plateau** is an area used for grazing animals and some farming. It gets very hot, especially in the spring and summer, when temperatures can soar to 113°F (45°C), causing the ground to become dry and cracked.

The huge Himalaya Mountains are named in Sanskrit, an ancient Indian language. The word Himalaya means "home of snow."

9

Above, a traditional snake charmer Left, harvesting marigolds

INDIA
WONDER

The Taj Mahal in Agra was built in the years between 1632 and 1653. Buried beneath it are the bodies of the ruler Shah Jehan and his wife, for whom this wonder was built.

**Above, silk saris
Right, Lakshminarayan,
a Hindu temple
Opposite, the Taj Mahal**

While most of India has a hot, **tropical** climate, the northern part of the country has cold, snow-capped peaks all year long. In fact, India has only three seasons, not four.

Winter lasts from October to February. Average temperatures are about 80°F (26°C), and very little rain falls. Spring lasts from March to May and can be the hottest time of the year. Not only are temperatures very hot, but it seldom rains during the spring season.

INDIA

SWIM

In the Bay of Bengal, whole herds of elephants have been known to swim from island to island.

Top right, bathing elephants in a river
Bottom right, water buffalo grazing in a lake
Below, stone statue of a sacred bull

Summer, lasting from June to September, is also hot. During this season **monsoons** sweep across the country from the **equator**, where they pick up moisture over the Indian Ocean. Usually hitting the southern part of the country first, they then move northward. All of the rain that comes with a monsoon soaks most of the country and often causes serious floods in cities and villages.

WETLAND WILDLIFE

Gangetic dolphins

Three species of otter

Three species of wildcat

Five species of marine turtle

Eight species of kingfisher birds

20 varieties of mangrove trees

Sundarbans crocodiles

13

Overall, most of the land in India is dry. In fact, the monsoons provide the country's only rainfall each year. One of India's driest places is the Thar Desert in the northwest. This region receives as little as two inches (5 cm) of rain each year. During the hot months, the land is baked by temperatures of up to 118°F (48°C).

Left, in the desert, camels are often used for transportation—even by mail carriers
Above, the rare Indian rhinoceros

INDIA
MYSTERY

In Delhi there stands a 1,600-year-old iron pillar that rises 23 feet (7 m) straight up. No one can explain why it has never rusted.

Above, traditional puppets from Rajasthan, India
Right, detail of the Taj Mahal

CITIES AND VILLAGES

India's big cities are much like other cities in the world, filled with tall office buildings, museums, and universities. Many of the cities are hundreds of years old. It is common to see a towering skyscraper next to an ancient temple. The people living there are either rich or extremely poor. Those who are wealthy live in fancy apartments, drive cars, and can give their children a good education. Those who are very poor may have to live on the street and beg for food.

India's cities are overcrowded, and along with the beautiful skyscrapers are horrible slums. It is estimated that nearly half of all the people of India live in poverty. Slums crowd many people in a one-room building; even worse, many people have no home at all. Many cannot find jobs, so they have no way to better their lives. Fortunately, since the 1970s, India's government has been working to build better housing for its people.

INDIA
DISASTER

In September 1993, an earthquake shook the Indian state of Maharashtra. In just a matter of seconds, more than 9,700 people were killed.

INDIA
TIGER

Bengal tigers grow a winter coat, which they shed in summer. They rest during the day and hunt at night, eating as much as 55 pounds (25 kg) of meat at one meal.

Meenakshi Temple

15

INDIA

Above, traditional wedding dress and jewelry
Right, Victoria Memorial in Calcutta

Three-fourths of India's people live in small villages. The homes are nothing more than huts made of mud and straw, and are often crowded together. Occasionally, a home is made of brick, a sign of wealth in a village. More than half a million of these villages exist throughout the country, and each one has unique features.

Some villages are farming communities; those near water are usually fishing villages. Other villages may be home to potters, weavers, or shopkeepers. Most of the village homes have no electricity or running water. To bring water into the home, the women take buckets to a well and carry them back on top of their heads. At night, the homes are lit by lanterns, though some villages have access to electricity nearby.

INDIA
PARTY

For a wedding feast, many Indians prepare fancy foods and wrap them in a layer of silver so thin that it can be eaten.

INDIA
HISTORY

*Scientists now know that around 2500 B.C. one of the earliest organized and **literate** civilizations in the world began in what is now India.*

INDIA

DRESSES

Indian women wear dresses, called saris, *made of one long piece of cloth that is wrapped around the body a certain way.*

INDIA

RELIGION

Around the first millennium B.C., *a great world religion called Buddhism first arose in India. This religion has since spread across much of Asia.*

Women in saris

A one-room schoolhouse can be found in some villages. School is free for Indian children between the ages of 6 and 14. However, most village children attend only the first few years of school. Often they are needed by the family to help earn money for food and clothing.

Alarge number of India's population are **vegetarians**. The few people who do eat meat usually eat only chicken or lamb. Indians eat many grains and vegetables. The grain is ground into flour and baked into flat breads, similar to pancakes. Many Indian meals are flavored with zesty spices, such as curry. It may be used with fish, eggs, or vegetables and served with rice. Dessert often includes fresh fruit, yogurt, and nuts.

INDIA
CROPS

A large type of fruit from India, called jackfruit, can reach lengths of three feet (0.9 m) and weigh up to 80 pounds (36 kg).

19

**Above, jackfruit
Left, picking tea leaves**

INDIA

Hills on the southern tip of India are known as the Blue Hills because they are always covered by a thin, blue mist.

Above, the oldest shrine in India, built in the third century B.C. Right, fruit stand in the city of Agra

India is able to grow most of the foods its people eat, though farmers must **irrigate** their fields often. Rice is the largest crop grown. In fact, the only country that grows more rice than India is China. Many of the crops farmers grow are sold to other countries. These are called **cash crops**. India leads the world in growing tea, **millet**, peanuts, cashews, peas, beans, and also in producing spices, such as pepper and ginger. Other major crops are bananas, apples, oranges, and potatoes.

INDIA
BIRDS

Every year, nearly 1,500 pelicans form breeding colonies near Madras. It is the largest gathering of pelicans in Asia.

Mounted guard at Rashtrapti Bhavan in Delhi, the home of the nation's president

INDIA

HONEY

Indians who live in the rain forests climb trees—up to 130 feet (40 m) high—to collect honey from wild bee hives.

Above, a barasingha, or swamp deer
Right, a peacock

The national animal of India is the Bengal tiger, which is why India is sometimes called "The Land of the Tiger." The borders of the country are filled with a wide variety of animals, some of which are very rare. In the Himalayas, snow leopards and ibex can be found.

The rain forests are home to elephants, monkeys, and many kinds of reptiles, such as the chameleon and the flying lizard. The desert is where a large population of camels lives.

Birds of all colors and sizes make India their home. Pelicans and crows are quite common, as are many types of vultures, including the large griffin. Golden eagles soar through India's skies, and for a magnificent splash of color there are flamingos, peacocks, and many species of pheasants.

INDIA
RARE

India is home to the world's rarest monkey, the lion-tailed macaque. Fewer than 4,000 still exist.

INDIA
LIZARD

India's flying lizards have been recorded gliding through the air as far as 115 feet (35 m).

Left, the slender loris (top) and black-faced langur monkey (bottom) live deep in India's rain forests

INDIA

TIGER

The Sundarbans Tiger Reserve is a 1,000-square-mile (2,560 sq km) area in India that offers protection to about 350 of these powerful cats.

INDIA

SNAKE

The largest poisonous snake in the world, the king cobra, lives on India's forest floor. One bite from this snake can kill a baby elephant.

Right, rhesus monkey
Far right, Indian cobra
Opposite, Bengal tiger

In fact, more than 1,000 different kinds of birds live in India. The ancestors of many species flew south from China thousands of years ago. Finding safety and plenty of food, the birds made India their new home.

INDIA
FACT

Indian elephants are smaller than African elephants; both have average life spans of 60 to 70 years.

Indian elephant

Unfortunately, many animals in India are **endangered**. To help with their survival, the government has set up more than 100 protected areas where animals cannot be hunted. The one-horned rhinoceros, Bengal tiger, and black panther are some of the animals that benefit from these protected areas. Another is the Asian lion. Less than 200 of these animals remain in the world. With the help of concerned people, there is hope that one day the population of these and other endangered species will increase.

INDIA
COWS

*Cows are **sacred** in India. Milk and a kind of butter called ghee are used only during religious ceremonies.*

INDIA
SWAMP

India's Sundarbans wilderness is a maze of rivers and streams around thousands of tiny islands. Running for 160 miles (256 km), this area contains one of the largest mangrove forests in the world.

Camel racing draws large crowds of spectators to outdoor tracks

TEAM PLAYERS

Many of India's people love to watch and play team sports. When other countries play India's national teams, all of the seats in the stadiums are filled, and radios and televisions all over the country are tuned-in to find out who will win. Field hockey is especially popular.

INDIA

FACT

On the average, about 70,000 babies are born each day in India. That's nearly 50 per minute.

INDIA

BAZAAR

Every Indian city has a huge market, called a bazaar, where almost anything can be bought— from food and jewels to dental services.

Camel halters

The game is similar to ice hockey, except that it's played outdoors on grass instead of on ice. India's teams are so skilled that they often win the gold medal in the Summer Olympic Games.

Some modern sports actually originated in India and then spread to other countries. One such sport is polo. In 1862, some British army officers saw Indians playing a horseback game called *pulu* and tried it themselves. They took the game back to England, and today, polo is one of that nation's favorite sports.

B adminton also came from India. It was originally called *poona*. An earl from England was visiting India and learned how to play. When he went back home, he taught others who were eager to learn. Because the name of the earl's estate was Badminton, the game was given that name.

In India, kite flying is considered a sport. Using great skill, kite flyers compete to try to knock other kites out of the sky.

INDIA
FACT

Camel bridles are hooked into the nose of the camel because the animal is constantly chewing.

Camels are often outfitted with colorful harnesses and blankets

Many Indians believe that the Ganges River is holy, and to take a dip in it will remove their sins.

INDIA
CLOTH

India is the second-largest cotton producer in the world. This nation is also famous for its beautiful silk cloth.

Right and opposite, many Indian stone carvings depict sacred animals and Hindu gods and goddesses

30

INDEPENDENT INDIA

Over the centuries, India has been claimed by many different nations. During the 1700s, the country became a British territory and remained that way until 1947. An important Indian leader was Mohandas Ghandi. He encouraged all of India to protest British rule in a peaceful manner. He was so loved by the people that they named him Mahatma, which means "great soul." India finally won its independence, but it would have to struggle through enormous challenges to survive. For example, in 1947, just 15 percent of the people could read and write, there were food shortages, and few jobs existed for people.

Today, the conditions in India have greatly improved. Now more than half the population can read and write, and farmers are producing bigger and better crops. Many people are still not able to find work, but more and more factories are being built in the cities. These developments will give people the jobs they need. Most importantly, they will give the nation of India hope for the future.

Glossary

Cash crops are foods that are grown especially to be sold to other countries for money.

Dialects are variations of an established language that are spoken in various areas of a country.

Endangered animals are threatened with becoming so few in number that their kind will suffer extinction, dying out completely and disappearing from Earth.

The **equator** is the dividing line between the northern and southern halves of the earth.

Fertile land has many qualities that allow plants to grow large in size and quantity.

To **irrigate** land is to bring water to it from another place, such as a river or a lake. The water may be carried through a system of pipes or on trucks.

People who are **literate** are able to read written words.

Millet is a type of grass with small seeds that are eaten.

Monsoons are very strong winds that change direction depending on the season; they usually bring a lot of rain or snow, and they can be devastating to any place they hit.

A **peninsula** is an area of land with water on three sides.

Plains are large areas of level, treeless land.

A **plateau** is an area of level land that is raised up from surrounding lands.

Rain forests receive more than 100 inches (254 cm) of rainfall each year. They are made up of broad-leafed evergreen trees and have a warm, humid climate. The climate encourages the trees to grow very tall, which shelters a great diversity of plant and animal life.

Things that are **sacred** are considered holy, meaning that they have important religious value to people.

A **tropical** climate is hot, with sticky, moist air.

Vegetarians are people who do not eat the meat of animals.

Index